Lakewood Memorial Library

IN MEMORY OF

Margaret P. "Peg" Wright

PRESENTED BY

Leslie W. Gray

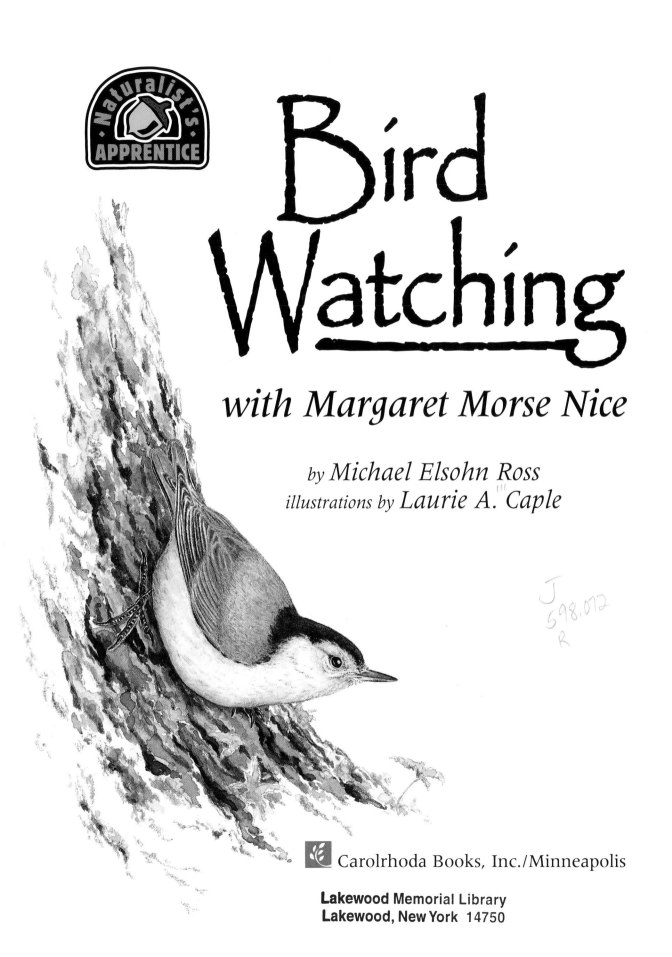

Bird Watching

with Margaret Morse Nice

by Michael Elsohn Ross
illustrations by Laurie A. Caple

Carolrhoda Books, Inc./Minneapolis

To Nalani and Timmy — M.E.R.

To my husband, Jim, who loves birds and works to protect them — L.A.C.

Many thanks to Dr. David DeSante, of the Institute for Bird Populations, for reviewing the manuscript and for his enthusiasm. Thanks also to Molly M. Henke, master bander at the Dodge Nature Center, St. Paul, Minnesota.

Text copyright © 1997 by Michael Elsohn Ross
Illustrations copyright © 1997 by Laurie A. Caple

All photographs courtesy of Natural Heritage/Natural History except: p. 30, Ken Boyer; p. 42, Joan Hochbaum; p. 44, Smithsonian Institution #87-9435; p. 46, Mount Holyoke College Archives and Special Collections. Song notes on p. 36 and drawings on pp. 33 and 40 courtesy of Dover Publications.

Carolrhoda Books, Inc. c/o The Lerner Publishing Group
241 First Avenue North, Minneapolis, MN 55401 U.S.A.

LIBRARY OF CONGRESS CATALOGING-IN-PUBLICATION DATA

Ross, Michael Elsohn, 1952–
    Bird watching with Margaret Morse Nice / by Michael Elsohn Ross ; illustrations by Laurie A. Caple.
        p.   cm. - (Naturalist's apprentice)
    Summary: Chronicles the life and career of ornithologist Margaret Morse Nice, who devoted more than eighty years to studying and writing about birds. Also includes tips and activities for readers to become bird watchers in their own right.
    Includes index.
    ISBN 1-57505-002-1
    1. Bird watching—Juvenile literature. 2. Nice, Margaret Morse, b. 1883—Juvenile literature. [1. Bird watching. 2. Nice, Margaret Morse, b. 1883. 3. Ornithologists. 4. Women—Biography.] I. Caple, Laurie A. ill. II. Title. III. Series: Ross, Michael Elsohn, 1952–   Naturalist's apprentice.
QL677.5.R65 1997   96-13876
598'.07234—dc20
Manufactured in the United States of America
1 2 3 4 5 6 – JR – 02 01 00 99 98 97

RED-WINGED BLACKBIRD (FEMALE)

Contents

AMERICAN ROBIN

Chapter 1
Feathered Treasures

Can you remember the last time you watched a bird? Perhaps you saw one soar over the trees or dive-bomb a cat. Maybe you witnessed a robin searching for a worm or a baby bird learning to fly. When you watched them, did you wonder just a little? Did you wonder how a robin finds worms, or why a little bird pesters big, fierce cats? Do you have questions about what you saw? Imagine spending eighty years following your questions. Picture yourself becoming one of the most amazing bird watchers of all time.

Over one hundred years ago, in 1893, nine-year-old Margaret Morse began to keep notes on all the strange and interesting things she noticed about birds. The first bird she described in her diary was the song sparrow. Little did she know that her interest in this bird would one day make her a famous **ornithologist,** a scientist who studies birds.

COMMON
YELLOWTHROAT
(MALE)

Luckily for Margaret, her parents encouraged their children to explore the wonders of nature. The Morses' home, in Amherst, Massachusetts, was surrounded by a lush orchard and garden. Here Margaret caught bugs, snakes, and other creatures. At a nearby pond, she and her little brother, Harold, scooped up water animals and studied them in an aquarium they had made from a dishpan. Like real **naturalists,** people who study nature, they investigated every wild thing they could find.

The Morse home was a fun place for young explorers. Each of the seven children had their own garden plot to plant as they wished. Every Sunday the whole family went for a wild romp in fields and forests around Amherst. Their father, Anson Morse, shared his love of plants. Their mother, Margaret Ely Morse, taught them the names of flowers and trees. But it was birds, not plants, that captured young Margaret's heart.

One day she sighted an unusual bright yellow bird with a black mask. Margaret felt as if she had discovered buried treasure! She wondered what the bird was called and searched excitedly through a book on common backyard birds. Not all entries in the book included drawings, so she guessed from the written descriptions that the bird was a hooded warbler. Much later, she found she'd been wrong—it was a yellowthroat—but that didn't dampen her excitement for birding.

Choosing and Using a Field Guide

Bird watchers nowadays have a different problem than young Margaret Morse. Rather than a lack of bird guides, there are shelves full of guides to choose from. Here are some features that will be helpful in unmasking the identity of your feathered friends.

✔ **Illustrations vs. Photos**
Believe it or not, a drawing or painting usually shows more detail than a photo. Go for a book with illustrations.

✔ **The Whole Gang**
Find a book that includes all the **species**, or kinds, of birds that live in your region, not just the common ones. Otherwise you'll be clueless when an uncommon bird pays a visit.

✔ **User-Friendly**
Choose a guide that is easy to use. If pictures and descriptions are all on one page, you'll be better able to make a quick ID while the bird is still in sight.

✔ **In the Pocket**
A book that can fit in your back pocket or belt pouch is just the right size. Imagine trying to use binoculars when you are carrying a book in your hand, or having to dig your guide out of your backpack every time you see a bird. Birds don't wait around for bird watchers to get their act together!

✔ **Get the Facts**
The first few times you go bird watching, simply flip through your field guide until you find a picture that matches each bird you see. As you become more familiar with your guide and the birds around you, you might recognize a bird as a member of the crow, sparrow, hawk, or other family. Then you'll be able to turn right to that section of the guide. Keep the book in a handy place where you can flip through it regularly. Soon you'll be able to make lightning-quick identifications.

✔ **Check Out a Checklist**
One problem with field guides is that they usually cover a large region, such as the East Coast or even all of the United States or Canada. While this feature may come in handy on trips to other places, it's hard to tell from the general descriptions whether or not a particular bird lives in your area. The solution to this problem is to use a checklist of local birds along with your bird guide. A checklist will help you narrow down the list of possibilities. For example, your guide might indicate that five different species of hawks live in your state, but your local checklist shows only one whose **range** includes your area. Checklists are usually available from local bird clubs, nature centers, and parks.

Another day, Margaret and Harold found a robin's nest and made a plan to mark the babies so the children would be able to tell the **brood,** or group of babies, from others in the neighborhood. Alas, when she and Harold reached the tree armed with a brush, paint box, and water, the young robins had already flown.

On Christmas Day 1895, when Margaret was twelve years old, she was thrilled to find a book called *Birdcraft* under the tree. Inside it were color drawings of hundreds of birds, both common and uncommon. Now she could learn about the yellow bird with the black mask and other backyard songsters. She read and reread *Birdcraft* as closely as a kid studying baseball cards.

Not long after, while playing in the attic, she found another thin book called *An Artificial Key to the Birds of Amherst.* This booklet was a list of birds she could expect to find in her own area. Now Margaret had the tools for identifying many of the birds she would meet on her bird-watching adventures.

In August 1896, Margaret's ten-year-old brother, Harold, died in a swimming accident. As the Morses drove their carriage to the cemetery to choose Harold's burial plot, Margaret spied some warblers heading south for the winter. Her instant thought was, "I must tell Harold." Then, with great sadness, she realized she could never again tell him anything.

After Harold's death, Margaret spent even more time bird watching and note keeping. Fortunately for Margaret, her older sister Sarah also became interested in birds. However, it wasn't wild ones that caught Sarah's fancy. She wanted to study the family's brown leghorn hens. How many eggs could a hen lay in a day?

Which hen laid the most? Sarah insisted that, like real scientists, they keep exact records on the number of eggs the hens produced. The chickens were no longer just farm animals and pets. They were the girls' laboratory subjects.

Sarah invented a system of one-way entrances to the hens' laying pen. The hens could go in by themselves but had to wait for one of the girls to let them out. As the girls released the birds, they tallied the number of eggs laid.

Margaret also took notes on the relationships between the hens. "Rexie bossed Prexie, Prexie bossed Queerie but, amusingly enough, Queerie pecked Rexie," wrote Margaret. More than thirty years later, she read an article on a newly studied behavior among hens called peck order—the way hens peck at each other to determine who's boss. It seemed odd to Margaret to be reading a scientific report on something she had noticed as a girl.

Margaret's peck-order study was an early sign of her eagle eyes. Unfortunately, not all birds are as easy to spy on as the leghorn hens were. Most bird watching requires binoculars, and using binoculars takes practice.

BROWN LEGHORN HENS

Choosing and Using Binoculars

Binoculars have become less expensive and easier to operate than they were when Margaret was a girl, but unless you know how to use them properly, they won't be of much value. Below are some hints to help you focus on the subject at hand.

✔ Best Binoculars

If you need to purchase or borrow binoculars, choose a pair that has a center focus—a focusing ring or lever located between the two eyepieces. Binoculars come in a variety of sizes and magnifications. The ideal magnifications for birding are 8 x 35 or 8 x 40. Standard-size binoculars are better than compact ones, because they are easier to hold steady.

✔ On the Dot

Most binoculars have an eyepiece adjuster. This numbered ring is found on one of the eyepieces. To adjust it, look through the binoculars and move the ring until you have a clear view with both your eyes. Leave the ring at that setting and note the number that is lined up with the dot. This is the setting that you should always use.

✔ Fast Draw

Birds are usually on the move, and bird watchers must learn how to focus quickly to keep them in view.

To become fast on the draw, try this outdoor exercise.

1. With your naked eye, look around until you see something far away with letters or numbers on it, such as a license plate or street sign.
2. Keep looking at it and, without moving your eyes or head, bring the binoculars up to your eyes. If you hold the binoculars level, you should see the object immediately. Then adjust the focus to read the letters. If this doesn't work, try again and concentrate on keeping your eyes and head locked in position and your binoculars level.
3. Practice to improve your speed, and then try to watch some moving objects such as dogs, squirrels, people, or even birds. When watching birds, always remember to search for them with your naked eye first. If you try to look for a bird through binoculars without having first located it with your naked eye, finding one may be a difficult and dizzying experience.

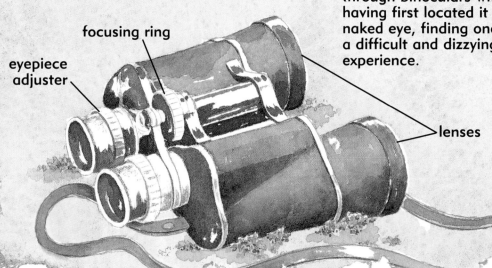

focusing ring

eyepiece adjuster

lenses

In July 1897, while thirteen-year-old Margaret was visiting at her grandparents' farm in Connecticut, she and her younger cousin Dick became expert tree climbers. Margaret's arms got scraped and scratched, but that didn't bother her. She swayed high in the branches and enjoyed her bird's-eye view.

Margaret's father, upon hearing of her climbing, wrote a letter advising her to behave in a more ladylike manner. Margaret wrote back, "If all the books about training daughters don't mention tree-climbing and out-of-doors exercise, I ought to write one myself. I think a girl ought to know how to ride, drive [a horse], climb, swim, row, cook, sew, do general housework, take walks, and have a good many pets."

ROSE-BREASTED GROSBEAK (MALE)

Chapter 2
Bird Detective

I wish I could help Nature, make people love Nature more," Margaret told her brother Will when he asked what she wanted to do in life. She also planned to explore the world and choose a profession outside the home. This did not fit with her parents' idea that she become a perfect homemaker.

Fortunately for Margaret, her "old-fashioned" parents thought a college education was good training for a future housewife. In 1901, Margaret entered Mount Holyoke, a college just for women. Here she found other young women who shared her love of nature. Students had no classes on Wednesdays, and Margaret spent them on all-day outings with friends. They were energetic hikers, and often they would hike thirty or forty miles in a single day!

In Margaret's time, girls weren't supposed to behave like boys, and women were not allowed the freedom of men. Women could not vote, nor were they free to dress as they pleased. Margaret's father, who taught history at Amherst College, had told her about a woman who visited his class dressed in men's clothes. The woman, Dr. Mary Edwards Walker, had been a surgeon during the Civil War. She believed it was unhealthy for women to wear tight corsets and long, heavy skirts. As an example to other women, she wore a more comfortable outfit: men's trousers, shirt, and jacket. Unfortunately that was against the law. She was continually tossed into jail, but Dr. Walker failed to give in. No doubt Margaret was envious, since she had to do her hiking in long skirts and starched blouses.

Like other young women, Margaret had always been discouraged from exploring the outdoors unless she had one of her brothers or an older man along to protect her from any wild animals or dangerous people she might meet. Even when she was in college, Margaret's parents worried about her hiking without an escort. Margaret reasoned that a gun offered just as much protection as a man did. And despite her father's objections, she bought a revolver to carry on solo expeditions. You don't need a firearm for bird watching, but many other items can be helpful.

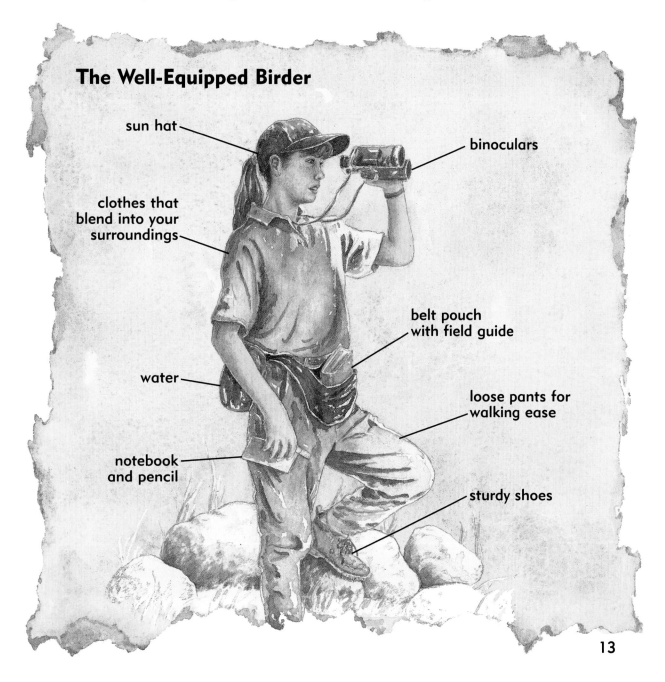

The Well-Equipped Birder

sun hat

binoculars

clothes that blend into your surroundings

belt pouch with field guide

water

loose pants for walking ease

notebook and pencil

sturdy shoes

Margaret's science classes were taught by brilliant women like Dr. Cornelia Clapp, who was one of the most famous zoologists, or animal scientists, of her time. But Margaret's classroom studies didn't thrill her like her nature explorations did. Lessons on rocks, plants, and animals—including birds—were interesting, but she could see very few connections to the wild things she loved. And classes conducted in the laboratory were as lifeless as the dead animals she was required to dissect. She found her foreign language studies much more rewarding and earned a degree in French in 1906.

After graduation, Margaret returned home. But she felt as if she had lost her way. She was only twenty-two years old, and she did not want to be a housewife. She wasn't interested in laboratory science or teaching either.

During the summer of 1907, Margaret attended two lectures by Dr. Clifton Hodge, of Clark University, and she knew she had found her path. Unlike other biologists who collected and dissected dead animals, Dr. Hodge studied live ones. He watched what they did and kept track of what they ate. Eagerly Margaret shared with him her desire to learn about live animals.

The Morse family in 1903. Front row: Anson, Sarah, Edward, Katharine, William, and Margaret. Back row: Margaret's parents, Margaret and Anson

Although her parents wished she'd stay at home, Margaret finally won their approval. Margaret enrolled at Clark University in the fall. There she discovered that "the world was full of problems crying to be solved." Dr. Hodge proposed that she study some bobwhite quail he was raising on his farm. These wild relatives of the domestic chicken were **endangered,** or close to dying out, because of overhunting, and it was important for biologists to prove that bobwhites were worth protecting.

Dr. Hodge believed the key to saving bobwhites was to figure out just what they ate. Like a mother bird, Margaret busily provided each bobwhite with a wide variety of bugs and weed seeds. She weighed each serving and carefully recorded every morsel that was munched. One day she watched a hen eat 700 bugs. Another day the same bird ate 1,532! Margaret estimated that a single bobwhite could eat 75,000 insects and five million weed seeds in one summer. This data showed how important bobwhites were in controlling the number of bugs and weeds on farms. Bobwhites could definitely be considered farmers' helpers.

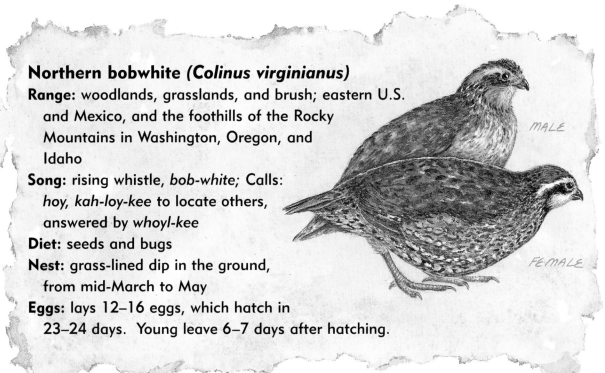

Northern bobwhite *(Colinus virginianus)*
Range: woodlands, grasslands, and brush; eastern U.S. and Mexico, and the foothills of the Rocky Mountains in Washington, Oregon, and Idaho
Song: rising whistle, *bob-white;* Calls: *hoy, kah-loy-kee* to locate others, answered by *whoyl-kee*
Diet: seeds and bugs
Nest: grass-lined dip in the ground, from mid-March to May
Eggs: lays 12–16 eggs, which hatch in 23–24 days. Young leave 6–7 days after hatching.

MALE

FEMALE

During her first summer of research, Margaret was adopted by a bobwhite chick whom she named Loti. As if she were his mother, Loti followed her everywhere, snuggling under her thick hair or strutting around the lab. When classes were over, Loti would burst out into the hall, calling in his loudest voice, "Bobwhite . . . bobwhite . . . bobwhite!"

Leonard Blaine Nice, a student in the lab across the hall, watched this show and set his sights on Margaret. Blaine was interested in birds too, and no doubt this didn't hurt his chances for romance. Soon he and Margaret were in love. In August 1909, Margaret and Blaine were married. Everyone was happy except Loti, who pecked at Blaine's toes whenever he could. Margaret gave up her studies at Clark to become a housewife. Cooking meals and cleaning their apartment were hard work, but she made time to write up the results of her study of bobwhites' diets. With Dr. Hodge's help, her article on bobwhites was published in 1910.

BOBWHITE CHICKS

One scientist who read Margaret's report complained about the use of caged birds to learn about the habits of wild bobwhites. Margaret knew he was right, but she still thought that the quantity of seeds and bugs she had witnessed being eaten was an important discovery. **Conservationists** agreed. They worked to protect all of nature and had been looking for the facts to prove the value of bobwhites. They were thrilled that she had proven that bobwhites were "worth" saving. Nature-study bulletins and magazines such as *Forest and Stream* used Margaret's data to highlight the bug-eating abilities of bobwhites. A political cartoon in the *Columbus Dispatch* entitled "Bugs or Birds—Ohio Can Have Its Choice" quoted Margaret's research and asked if Ohio could afford to allow the hunting of bobwhites. Finally Margaret had found a way to "help Nature."

Birdbrained Questions

Just because you have questions about birds doesn't mean you're a birdbrain. When Margaret realized scientists didn't have all the answers, she began to pay closer attention to her own questions. Have you ever thought of following some of those wild questions that pop into your own brain? Make a list of your questions in a special notebook. As you watch birds and learn more about them, review your questions. Maybe you'll have some answers—and some new questions.

AMERICAN TOAD

Imagine filling your yard with pet hens, frogs, toads, guinea pigs, and rabbits. In 1913, Blaine and Margaret moved to Norman, Oklahoma, where Blaine started a teaching job at the University of Oklahoma. Norman was on the edge of the prairie, and Margaret fell in love with the wildness. Animals brought home from Blaine's laboratory joined the hens and bees he and Margaret raised in their big backyard.

Margaret and daughter Eleanor, 1921

The Nices were now the parents of two daughters: three-year-old Constance and baby Marjorie. Like her own mother, Margaret shared her love of nature with her children. In addition to raising all kinds of pets, they went on walks through prairie wildflower gardens. Under big skies, they saw strange birds such as scissor-tailed flycatchers and burrowing owls.

Though Margaret was enchanted by the beauty of the prairie, caring for her daughters and the house gave her little time to study nature seriously. So in an effort to satisfy her longing for research, she decided to study Constance and Marjorie. Fascinated with their behavior, she took notes on their speech and vocabulary. In 1915—the same year a third daughter, Barbara, was born—Margaret published her first scientific paper on language development. She was thirty-two years old.

Three years later, daughter Eleanor came along. Both girls joined their big sisters as subjects of study.

18

RED-WINGED BLACKBIRD (MALE)

Changing diapers, cleaning house, and cooking. Life with four children was busy—too busy. Margaret loved her young daughters, yet she felt trapped in the life of a housewife. Sometimes she wished she could be free like a bird. Birds, she reasoned, are busy caring for young only a month or two a year. Then the youngsters grow up and leave home, and the adults have a vacation from parenting until they mate again the next spring.

As her daughters grew, Margaret had more freedom to explore nature. Before long, Constance and Blaine could watch the younger girls and Margaret could go on short walks by herself. One day in 1919, while sitting by the Canadian River, she reviewed her situation. "I saw that for many years I had lost my way. I had been led astray on false trails and had been trying to do things contrary to my nature. I resolved to return to my childhood vision of studying nature and trying to protect the wild things of the earth."

Margaret chose nearby Snail Brook for her classroom. One cold December day, she decided to start a list of the kinds of birds she saw and to note how many of each kind she saw or heard. As winter turned to spring, more and more birds came to make their homes in the tangled vines along the brook.

Margaret counted the numbers of red-winged blackbirds, robins, sparrows, and even green-winged teal. Regardless of whether she went alone or with her girls, she always kept notes. Blaine helped too, and soon their list was long. In fact, it became so long that Margaret and Blaine turned it into a 224-page book called *The Birds of Oklahoma*, which would be published in 1924. At age thirty-six, Margaret had once again filled her life with birds.

Keeping a List

How many kinds of birds do you think you could see in your neighborhood? The only way to find out is to keep a list. Invite your family members to record their sightings too. How many different species do you think you'll see after a week, a month, a year? Margaret and Blaine Nice had no idea when they started their list that it would turn into a book. Who knows what your list might turn into!

BLUE JAY

NORTHERN CARDINAL
(FEMALE)

DOWNY WOODPECKER
(MALE)

MOURNING DOVE

Chapter 3
The Watcher at the Nest

Mourning doves had been protected from hunting in Oklahoma from 1913 to 1917. But after that, dove hunting was made legal again. And in 1919, the state game warden announced plans to open the hunting season earlier than it had ever been opened before—in early to mid-August. He claimed that doves were finished nesting by then.

Margaret disagreed. She believed that doves nested through September and that hunting should be delayed until the adults were finished caring for their young. Like a detective, she set out to gather evidence. For the next couple of months, she and her daughters hunted everywhere for dove nests. When they found one, Constance would clamber up the tree and report on the contents while her mother made notes. One time, Margaret decided to let four-year-old Barbara help. After she was boosted up to a nest, Margaret asked her what was in it.

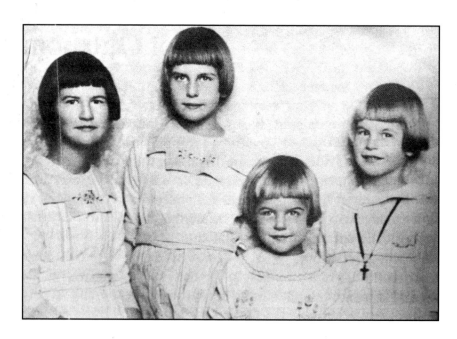

Constance, Marjorie, Eleanor, and Barbara

"One egg and one vat (rat)," answered Barbara.

"What?" Margaret asked in astonishment.

"One egg and a mouse?" the little girl answered more tentatively.

"What do you see?" Margaret asked again.

"One egg and one *baby bird,*" Barbara finally answered, triumphant. To someone who had never seen a **nestling,** or newborn, the little creature didn't even look like a bird!

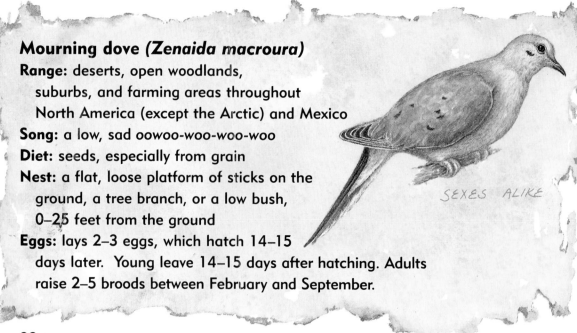

Mourning dove (Zenaida macroura)

Range: deserts, open woodlands, suburbs, and farming areas throughout North America (except the Arctic) and Mexico

Song: a low, sad oowoo-woo-woo-woo

Diet: seeds, especially from grain

Nest: a flat, loose platform of sticks on the ground, a tree branch, or a low bush, 0–25 feet from the ground

Eggs: lays 2–3 eggs, which hatch 14–15 days later. Young leave 14–15 days after hatching. Adults raise 2–5 broods between February and September.

SEXES ALIKE

Blaine and Margaret with their youngest daughters, Eleanor (left) and Janet

In August, the Nices found nestlings in fourteen nests, and in September they counted twenty-eight more. But their most important discovery was that three of them weren't empty until October. Margaret reported her discovery to the local newspaper and shared her evidence with the Oklahoma Game Department and the U.S. Biological Survey. Presented with the facts, the warden chose not to open dove hunting until October, when nesting was done.

In 1923, Margaret gave birth to her fifth daughter, Janet. For the next few years, being a mother kept her too busy to continue her bird studies. But during a summer visit to her parents' home in 1925, she finally had a chance to spend some time watching birds again.

On the evening of June 18, after a stroll in the woods, she heard an unfamiliar song and went off in search of the singer. Before seeing him, she caught a glimpse of a silent female magnolia warbler with nesting material in her beak.

"She dives into a white pine. I wait and see the performance repeated. The male in the meantime is singing, but not coming into sight. Finally a little bird comes rustling out of the juniper [tree] nearest to me. After that apparently the warblers went to sleep, but the mosquitoes did not."

Margaret was not bothered by pesky mosquitoes or secretive birds. She returned the next morning and discovered a half-built nest hidden on a branch of the juniper. Six days later, the nest held three eggs. After another five days, she found something else. "The nest contains the tiniest babies I have ever seen—three wee blind orange-red infants, naked except for a few tiny tufts of black down," she reported.

The following morning, Margaret sat herself down in a chair near the juniper and watched the warblers for several hours. Over the next eight days, she spent much of her time there, jotting notes on their behavior. At first only the female fed the young. But soon the male realized that the eggs had hatched and began to help with the feeding. All the while, he sang—up to 242 songs per hour! "Perched on the tippety-top of a red cedar, his little head bright blue in the sunshine, his breast a brilliant yellow splashed with black stripes, my Magnolia Warbler looked up to heaven and sang with all his might," wrote Margaret.

As the days passed, the father warbler began to bring home more juicy bugs for the babies than his mate did. Soon he was so caught up in his bug gathering that he practically stopped singing.

Magnolia warbler *(Dendroica magnolia)*
Range: hemlock spruce forests of northern and eastern U.S.
Song: "Pretty, pretty Rachel"
Diet: insects and spiders
Nest: a shallow, loose cup of coarse grasses and twigs, lined with fine roots and grass; usually on horizontal branches of spruce or fir trees, close to trunk, 1–35 feet above the ground. Nests May to June
Eggs: lays 3–5 white eggs with brown spots, which hatch 11–13 days later. Young leave 8–10 days after hatching.

MALE

FEMALE

Like the warbler parents, Margaret began to feel protective of the nestlings. She knew that red squirrels commonly eat young birds, and when she spied a red squirrel close to the nest, she was alarmed. Never before had she felt it was her duty to interfere. Now she felt differently. Fearing for the birds' lives, Margaret shot the squirrel.

After the shotgun blast, it's not surprising that the female warbler became a bit nervous about having Margaret around. For an hour, the bird continually chirped, "Tit, tit, tit," at Margaret. The warbler fed her young only three times and sat with them for only a couple of minutes. Though the nestlings seemed to be getting hungry, the mother paid more attention to Margaret, chipping loudly whenever she was near. During the next few days, the warbler parents took turns feeding their young and scolding Margaret.

On the morning of July 15, a disappointed Margaret found the nest empty. Most likely some other hungry hunter had found them. Perhaps then she realized the foolishness of interfering in nature. Years later, she remembered those twenty-six hours of watching in the woods as her "initiation into bird watching."

MAGNOLIA WARBLER
NESTLINGS

Hunting for Nests

Watching bird nests is a good sport for folks who like to sit in the shade and relax. The best time of year to spot an occupied nest is spring or early summer.

Supplies
binoculars
watch
notepad
pen or pencil

What to Do

✔ Pick a place where you've seen plenty of birds before, then sit or lie as quietly as a log. After a while, birds will most likely forget you are there and go about their business.

✔ Look for a bird carrying bugs or hauling sticks, string, straw, or any other material that might be used to build a nest. Often the bird will make many trips to the same place. Watch where it goes. Listen for a bird singing over and over again from the same location and try to see where it is. These birds are probably at or near their nests.

✔ Back off if a bird seems to notice you and moves about nervously, flicking its wings or tail and singing short, repetitive notes, or **calls.** You are most likely disturbing it. Find another watch post a little farther away and a little better hidden.

✔ Once you have seen a bird return to one spot many times, move closer and try to locate the nest. Since nests usually match their surroundings, they can be difficult to see. If you can't find the nest,

SOLITARY VIREO NEST

return to your watch post and observe the bird until you have a better view of where it is going.

✔ After finding a nest, move away quickly to prevent any disturbance that might scare the parents or their young. Pick a good place to watch the nest where the bird parents don't seem to notice you.

✔ Play it safe. Stay away from a nest if there are any egg eaters such as jays, crows, squirrels, or cats nearby. If the bird parents get excited by your presence, their alarm calls might lead the **predators** to the nest.

✔ Keep notes on what you see. How long does it take the birds to build the nest? What materials do they use? How many times an hour do the parents feed their young?

Chapter 4
The Birds Next Door

In 1926, Margaret's studies on the speech development of her children finally paid off. Clark University awarded the forty-two-year-old a master's degree in psychology. A year later, the Nices moved to Columbus, Ohio, where Blaine had taken a job at Ohio State University. Constance was now seventeen, Marjorie fourteen, Barbara twelve, Eleanor nine, and Janet four. They were sad to leave Snail Brook and the Oklahoma prairie. But Margaret was pleased with their new home, which sat on a bluff above the Olentangy River. A "great weed patch" flourished there, dotted with sunflowers, asters, and goldenrod. Since this neglected patch of land was located between two bridges, Margaret called it "Interpont," from the French words for "between bridges." Except for workers who were paid to clear plants from the riverbanks and a few boys who hunted birds, the Nices had Interpont all to themselves.

That winter, Margaret's life took a tragic turn when her daughter Eleanor caught pneumonia and died. To soften her sorrow, Margaret hid herself in her bird studies. In the spring of 1928, she began to watch a song sparrow whom she labeled 1M (the *M* is for "male") and affectionately called Uno. He and his mate lived in the Nices' backyard. Margaret caught them in a special cage and marked each of them by putting a small metal band on one ankle. Like little bracelets, these bands were stamped with a number so that she could tell them apart from other song sparrows if she caught them again.

Song sparrow (*Melospiza melodia*)
Range: areas with brushy cover and nearby water in southern Canada and the U.S.
Song: "Maids! Maids! Hang up your teakettle-ettle-ettle"; Calls: *chimp, tchunk, tchip*
Diet: insects, seeds, berries
Nest: a cup-shaped mixture of weeds, grasses, fine roots, and fine bark, lined with fine grass and sometimes horsehair. Usually built on the ground early in the season and later 2–4 feet up in weeds or shrubs
Eggs: lays 3–6 greenish white eggs with reddish brown markings, which hatch 12–13 days later. Young leave 10 days after hatching. Adults raise 2–3 broods between February and August.

SEXES ALIKE

On May 22, Margaret found Uno's nest with three eggs in it. Over the next 5 days, she kept watch for 18 hours. One egg hatched on the 28th and another the following day. Unfortunately, during the night of June 2, the babies disappeared.

Instead of discouraging Margaret, this experience made her more curious. She continued to watch Uno and other song sparrows as carefully as she had watched her captive bobwhites. In her notebooks, she wrote pages and pages of observations. Though the song sparrow is a common bird, her studies would make history. Margaret was watching free, living animals and studying them in more detail than any scientist before her.

Spying on Sneaky Little Birds

Just like a television soap opera, birds' days are full of drama. If you watch patiently and quietly, you will be rewarded with many fine shows. You may be able to do this from the comfort of your own home. Birds will seldom notice you if you post yourself at a window while they are busy outdoors. But to guarantee yourself a front-row seat, build a bird blind outside.

Supplies
large cardboard box (big enough for you to fit in comfortably)
stool or pillow
pen or pencil
scissors or sharp knife
notebook
snacks (optional)
video camera (optional)

What to Do

✔ Lay the box on its side and crawl in, facing the closed end. Find a comfortable position, either on a pillow or a stool.

✔ Look straight ahead and pick a spot on the box directly in front of you. Mark the spot and cut a hole 6 inches wide by 1 inch high (15 cm x 2.5 cm). Watch your fingers!

✔ Set the blind near a nest, feeding area, or other popular bird hangout. Stock it with a snack and a drink if you like, and don't forget a notebook and a pen or pencil for recording what you see.

✔ If you have a video camera, you can film the action from inside your bird blind. Just cut the lookout hole the size and shape of the camera lens. And make sure you get permission before you borrow someone else's equipment.

AMERICAN GOLDFINCHES (FEMALE)

PURPLE FINCH (MALE)

In order to get to know her sparrow neighbors, Margaret banded as many of them as she could. She caught adult birds in a special trap made with a funnel and baited with a mixture of seeds. After entering the broad part of the funnel, the birds squeezed through the narrow end to reach the food chamber. Once inside, they were unable to get back out. Before releasing the birds, Margaret weighed and measured them and assigned them names. In addition to numbered metal bands, Margaret started using different combinations of colored ankle bands so she would be able to identify a bird from a distance once it was released. By 1936 she had banded 517 adult song sparrows and 353 young!

After a bird was banded, Margaret kept track of its whereabouts. She discovered who mated with whom and where each bird spent its time. Some birds, like Uno, left for the winter, while other birds visited Interpont only during the wintertime. Still others passed through just during the spring and fall. Why did some birds fly south and others stay? Why was there all this coming and going?

Margaret kept records of all the birds and tried to solve this mystery. When she compared song sparrows that stayed all year with ones that lived at Interpont for only part of the year, the only difference she noticed was their color. All year-round residents were darker. But this, she realized, was the result of soot from the polluted air of Columbus. The more time birds spent in the area, the sootier and darker they became. Margaret had no other clues. She still didn't know why birds came and went when they did. Like most researchers, Margaret often ended up with more questions than she had started with.

Join the Bandwagon

American scientists keep tabs on bird numbers by sharing their findings on a database called MAPS (Monitoring Avian Productivity and Survivorship). Just as Margaret did, these bird watchers band birds using numbered metal bands supplied by the National Biological Service. This way, the same bird won't be counted twice. The information gathered on MAPS shows how problems like pollution and the loss of forests are affecting birds in North America.

How would you like to witness birds being banded? Around the United States, there are over three hundred licensed bird-banding stations that contribute data to MAPS. Many are operated by bird-loving individuals or nature centers. Like drivers, bird banders must have a license or work with someone who does. It is against the law to trap birds without this license, so forget any plans to make homemade bird traps! Instead, call The Institute for Bird Populations at (415) 663-1436 to find a bird-banding station in your area where you can watch licensed banders. If you are unable to make a long-distance call, send a self-addressed, stamped envelope along with your request to:

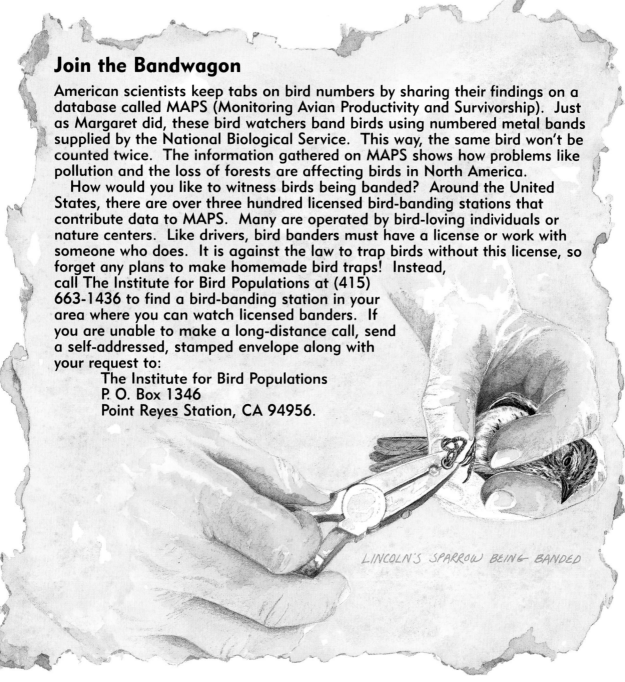

The Institute for Bird Populations
P. O. Box 1346
Point Reyes Station, CA 94956.

LINCOLN'S SPARROW BEING BANDED

Margaret often had repeat visitors to her banding station. This was no surprise to her, because she had observed that birds claim an area of land for their own each season. As she studied her song sparrows, she became familiar with how they set up these **territories.**

When male birds arrived at Interpont in late winter, they would begin to sing from certain treetops and shrubs. Each of these places, called a **song post,** marked a boundary of a bird's territory. The birds' songs were both a warning for other male birds to keep out and an invitation for female birds to come and mate with them. From these posts, each male guarded his land and chased away trespassers.

On March 9, 1929, Margaret discovered Uno near her house, in the same territory that he had occupied the year before. It was bounded on one side by a bluff and on the other side by rosebushes. These rosebushes separated Uno's territory from that of 4M, another male song sparrow. That same day, Margaret noticed that 4M was spreading out into Uno's territory and wondered if Uno would fight back.

The next morning, Margaret spied 4M and Uno on the ground. Feathers puffed out like pigeons, the two sparrows faced each other, but only Uno sang. First 4M tried darting

SONG SPARROW

at Uno, but Uno would back up only a tiny bit. Finally 4M attacked. The dust flew as the two birds pecked and scratched at each other. When the fight was over, each returned to one of his song posts and sang. Margaret figured out that 4M had given up on his invasion of Uno's territory.

For nearly a week, Margaret spent several hours a day watching the two song sparrows and listening to them sing and sing. Then suddenly the singing almost stopped. Instead of 260 songs per hour, they uttered only 3. She noticed Uno and 4M with an unbanded sparrow on the border between their territories. Even though 4M was acting fierce by puffing out his feathers, Uno blocked him from the stranger. After 4M finally left, Uno went near the strange bird, flipped its wings, and squawked, "Eee-eee-eee." Then Uno pounced, but still the stranger didn't leave. At first, Margaret was bewildered. But after a little more watching, she realized that the stranger was Uno's new mate. Margaret had just watched the song sparrow's **courtship** ritual. Instead of giving flowers or inviting the female song sparrow to dinner, Uno pounced on her to convince her that he was the best male for a mate.

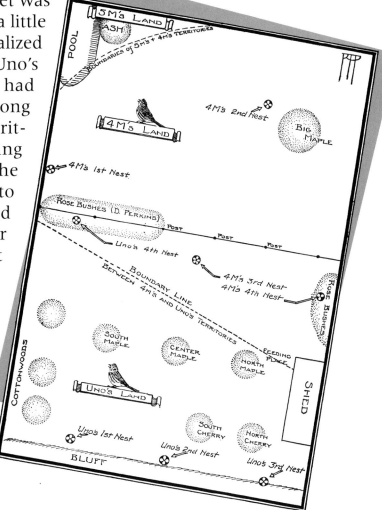

Margaret's map of Uno's and 4M's territories in 1929

33

Over the following years, Margaret mapped the territories at Interpont. She wondered why some birds claimed the same territory year after year, while others, like 4M, chose a different site almost every year. As always, there were many questions for which Margaret wanted to find answers.

Mapping Territories

Do you think you could find bird territories in your own neighborhood? If it's spring or summer and you've been hearing a lot of bird songs lately, chances are good that birds are guarding territories right outside your window.

Supplies
paper
pen or pencil
binoculars

What to Do

✔ To tune into territories, locate a singing bird and watch it for a while. Does it seem to sing from the same spots throughout the day? These are probably its song posts.

✔ Make a map of the area you are watching and mark the song posts on the map.

✔ With a little patience and luck, you will see your bird chasing another bird or being chased in return. These bird battles usually take place along territory borders. (Though bird fights often appear quite ferocious, birds usually escape from them a little upset but otherwise unharmed.) Mark the fight sites on your map.

✔ Connect the dots on your map, and you'll have a good map of the bird's territory.

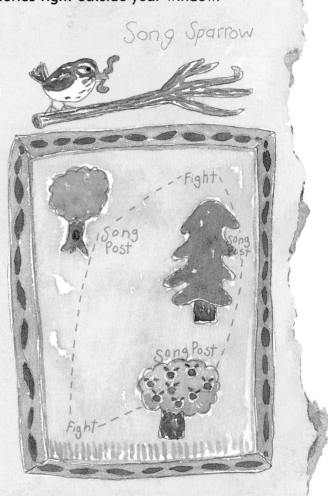
Song Sparrow
Fight
Song Post
Song Post
Song Post
Fight

Chapter 5
Weed Patch Songsters

Have you ever wondered how long a bird song lasts or how often a bird sings? Margaret did. She timed song sparrows and found out that most of their songs are only 2 to 3 seconds long. That's the same time it takes you to breathe in or out. No wonder a song sparrow can easily sing 5 to 7 songs in just 1 minute! Margaret even counted the number of songs 4M sang in a single day. From sunrise to sunset, he produced a whopping total of 2,305 songs!

Margaret became so good at listening to the elaborate pattern of notes in each song that she could tell one bird's songs from another's. Even from her bed, she could hear Uno and 4M and tell who was who. This was no simple trick, since a song sparrow may sing as many as twenty-four different variations of the same song sparrow tune. Like human musicians, song sparrows may perform the same basic tune in several different styles. For example, "Mary Had a Little Lamb" can be sung in a rap, punk, or jazz style, but it's still the same song.

Uno had six distinctive variations of the song sparrow's "Maids! Maids! Hang up your teakettle-ettle-ettle" song, while 4M had nine.

Margaret gave each variation a letter and described it in her notes using a code of dots, dashes, and curved lines. Here are a few of her descriptions:

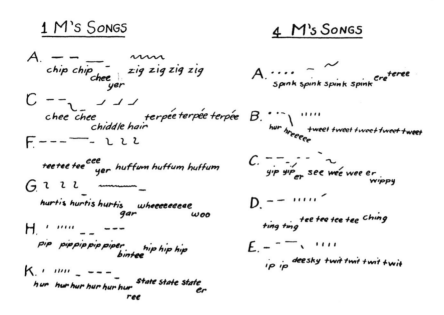

She also included a written description. "4M's song A had a determined, almost grim sound," she wrote one day. "With C he seemed in a desperate hurry; G was light and airy—a charming song; and K the prettiest of all, with the gayest little lilt at the end. Uno's H was uninspired, and his C had a triumphant ring, while F was clear, of exquisite haunting beauty."

Margaret knew from the research of other scientists that people can hear less than a third of the notes in a song sparrow's song. Nonetheless, Margaret kept notes on the birds' songs and calls and recorded their actions.

In most bird species, only the males sing, while both males and females produce a variety of calls. A call is usually a single note, while a song is a series of notes. Songs are repeated hour after hour by males who are defending territories or courting females. Calls, on the other hand, are repeated over a shorter period of time and are used to communicate a variety of messages. Most birds will pause between calls or songs.

After long hours of watching and listening to song sparrows' songs and calls, a remarkable thing happened to Margaret. She began to understand their language! Here are some of her interpretations of song sparrow calls:

Feeding: *see-see, kerr,* or *tit-tit-tit*
Announcing location: *eep* or *ick*
Threatening others: *zhee,* a growl
Fear: *tik*
Greeting mate: *ee-ee-ee,* a trill
Warning to other birds: *tchunk*
Worry (such as anxiety over young in nest): *tchip*
Pain: *weech*

Big Ears

You don't have to have big, floppy elephant ears to be a good listener. In fact, birds hear each other perfectly well, and their ears aren't even visible. Listening to birds is like hearing a new language. With practice, your ears will gradually tune in to a wonderful variety of songs and calls.

Supplies
notebook
pencil
watch
binoculars (optional)

What to Do
✔ Settle yourself in a spot where you can hear birds singing. Close your eyes (this may help you concentrate better) and listen carefully. Hold up a finger for each different call or song that you hear. How many different types of bird sounds do you hear during a few minutes of listening?

✔ Single out a bird to watch, and tally the number of times it sings in a minute (or longer if it sticks around). How many times do you think it would sing in an hour?

PURPLE FINCH (MALE)

Song Sparrow Trivia

✔ Sparrows increase their weight by 30 percent between the end of summer and January. That would be like a 100-pound kid gaining 30 pounds over the winter.

✔ Song sparrows are heavier in the afternoon than in the morning. Does your weight vary from morning to afternoon too?

✔ Though 4M was at least eight years old when he died, the average life span of a song sparrow is less than two years.

In 1936, Blaine took a job at the Chicago Medical School, so the Nices moved again. For the first time, Margaret was living in the middle of a big city. She no longer had song sparrows for neighbors, so she decided to raise some herself.

Loti, the bobwhite quail, had lived with Margaret and Blaine when they were first married. When the Nice girls were young, the family had adopted several orphaned mourning doves as pets. Now, with her children all grown, Margaret made room for song sparrows in her new house. Though they had cages, they were allowed to fly freely from room to room. One frequent visitor to the Nices' home commented that it was sometimes hard to carry on a dinner conversation when a sparrow hopped across his plate.

Margaret raised several broods and studied how they learned to sing, fly, and feed themselves. She discovered that young song sparrows can utter a simple warble at 13 days old without ever having heard an adult sparrow sing. However, it was necessary for them to hear an adult before they could learn a complete song.

Name That Tune

Consider how easy it is for you to recognize the tune of a favorite song. If you want to know bird songs or calls as well as you do the current Top 40, try some of these tricks.

✔ Find a spot where you can hear birds. Close your eyes and listen carefully. As you hear a call or song, point in the direction it's coming from. Open your eyes and look for the bird. (Use binoculars if you need to.) You may discover that there are several birds in different places giving the same call or song. To help you identify a bird, most field guides give short descriptions of songs and calls. Other field guides are written especially for identifying birds by the sounds they make.

✔ As you learn new bird songs, try to describe them as Margaret did. Here are several ways to describe sounds.

   1. Invent words to imitate the bird's call. A word made to imitate a sound is called onomatopoeia (ah-noh-mah-toh-PEE-ah). *Woof, quack,* and *crash* are examples of onomatopoeia. The names of some birds come from onomatopoeia for the songs they make. Chickadees get their name from their most common song, "Chick-a-dee-dee-dee."

   2. Create a phrase out of everyday words that remind you of the bird's call. The robin's song is often described as "Cheer up, cheer up, cheer up," while a yellow warbler's song can be written "Sweet, sweet, sweet, I'm so sweet."

3. Compare the birdcall to another sound that's more familiar to you. To some birders, a nuthatch's call sounds like the beep of a truck when it's backing up. A pine siskin's call sounds like a zipper.

4. Imagine what the birdcall would look like if you could see it. Really creative birders see images in their head when they hear a song. For example, the house wren might bring to mind cascading fireworks and the wren tit a bouncing ball.

✔ To really learn a song or call, simply look for the bird every time you hear it. After you have seen and heard the bird sing many times, remembering it will be a cinch. Once you learn to recognize a few voices, picking up new songs will be easier. Tapes or CDs of birdcalls are often available at the library and are useful in confirming the source of a call or song that you have heard before. However, trying to memorize bird songs from a recording can be frustrating, because a whole variety of songs are usually played one after another.

Chapter 6
New Adventures

During a long, solitary train trip in 1947, Margaret grew bored. To entertain herself, she started to sketch the trees she saw from her window. As a child, Margaret had taken drawing lessons, but she had stopped because she didn't think she was good at it. Now, at age sixty-three, she made an amazing discovery: drawing was fun! From that day on, she sketched and sketched. (The drawing on this page is one of Margaret's.) She even used her drawings of birds and plants to illustrate some of her articles and books.

Quick Draw
To sketch like Margaret, you don't have to wait fifty years. You don't have to wait until you get bored either. Not only is it fun, but it will help you learn to look at birds more closely.

Supplies
sketchbook, or scratch paper on a clipboard
colored pens, pencils, or crayons
pen or pencil
binoculars (optional)

What to Do

✔ Settle yourself at your favorite bird-watching post. Then set your sights on a single bird.

✔ Make a quick sketch of the shape of the bird by making one oval for the body and another oval for the head.

✔ Examine the shape of the bill, wings, legs, and tail. Add each to the rough sketch.

✔ Add any obvious color patterns that you notice.

✔ If you have time, try to make some quick sketches to show the bird in different positions, such as flying or hopping. Since birds are always on the move, you'll need to draw fast. Don't worry about it looking sloppy. Just get it down on paper. The more you practice, the easier it will be and the more details you'll see!

Great Blue Heron

Would you protest if you heard that an ancient forest was about to be logged or a wildlife park was going to become an army base? Would you say anything if you saw people destroying the homes of your neighborhood birds?

Throughout her life, Margaret came across birds in danger. In her early years as an ornithologist, she worked to protect bobwhites and mourning doves from hunters. To help song sparrows, she tried to stop plans to clear Interpont of its wild plants. But birds all over the United States were still being endangered by the actions of people. Something more needed to be done. In writing a bird book for the general public (rather than just for bird experts), Margaret saw a new opportunity to educate people about the importance of protecting birds.

The Watcher at the Nest is mostly about Margaret's bird studies, but she also used the book to share her protests against the misuse of land. She wrote about the dangers of overgrazing, overhunting, building highways, poisoning wildlife, and clearing bird habitats. In one exam-

Margaret and Blaine's daughter Constance accompanied them on many bird-watching trips, including this one to Manitoba, Canada, in 1953.

ple, she described how the Tulsa Audubon Society had saved a cypress grove in southern Oklahoma from logging. With its own money, the society bought the land and turned it into a preserve for the anhingas, egrets, and herons that nested there. Thirty years before the beginning of the environmental movement, Margaret was crusading for the earth.

Margaret didn't even mind battling the U.S. Army. In 1955, she wrote an article for *Nature Magazine* protesting plans for a guided-missile base in the Wichita Mountains Wildlife Refuge. Margaret also worked to keep army bases out of Jackson Park, in Chicago. Both efforts were successful. Working with others, she helped protect wild places such as Dinosaur National Monument, Indiana Dunes State Park, and groves of California's coast redwoods.

Though encouraged by these victories, Margaret was disappointed by her failure to influence farmers. The **pesticides** they used to kill insects and other crop-eating pests were poisoning many birds. "It is a constant battle to keep gains that protect a little of the earth from the hands of greed," wrote Margaret in her autobiography, *Research is a Passion with Me.*

Bird Gardens

Margaret would be pleased to see the progress in conservation efforts that followed America's first Earth Day in 1970. The U.S. government passed the Endangered Species Act, banned harmful pesticides such as DDT, and set aside more land for parks and wilderness areas. However, some species of birds are still in danger, both in the U.S. and all over the world.

Creating better bird habitats in your backyard or neighborhood is one way to help both birds and people. Birds need to nest where there is protection from predators. Trees, shrubs, and areas left to grow wild offer safe nest sites. A garden rich in seeds and bugs can provide all the food birds need. Here are some tips for turning a plot of land into a place for the birds.

✔ Plant a wide variety of flowers and berry bushes. Check with a nursery to see which species are native to your area. These will produce the greatest banquets of seeds and fruit.

✔ Don't use pesticides. Even brands that don't directly poison birds still kill bugs. Without bugs, most songbirds are unable to feed themselves or their young.

✔ Plant more trees, and leave dead trees standing whenever possible. Dead or alive, trees offer great nest sites.

✔ Build or buy and install birdhouses for hole-nesting birds. Set up bird baths in open areas where birds can keep an eye out for cats.

There's no doubt about it, Margaret Morse Nice had birdmania. In spite of prejudices against women becoming scientists, Margaret followed her desire to share her love of nature with the world. By the time she stopped writing in her eighties, she had published seven books, 250 journal and newspaper articles, and 3,133 reviews of other scientists' work. Experts everywhere recognized her contribution to science and considered her the founder of ethology, the study of animal behavior. Margaret spent her later years writing her autobiography, the story of her life with birds. She died in 1974 at the age of ninety, a few months after Blaine had passed away. *Research is a Passion with Me* was published after her death, in 1979.

Has Margaret's story infected you with birdmania? Grab a notebook and some binoculars and head outside. In no time, you'll be hopelessly hooked. Happy birding!

Janet, Margaret, and Constance, 1956

Important Dates

BOBWHITE FEATHER

December 6, 1883—Margaret Morse is born in Amherst, Massachusetts.

1896—Brother Harold dies

1901—Enters Mount Holyoke College

1906—Graduates from Mount Holyoke

1907—Enters Clark University. Loti, the bobwhite quail, is born.

1909—Marries Leonard Blaine Nice

1910—Daughter Constance is born

1913—Moves to Oklahoma. Daughter Marjorie is born

1915—Daughter Barbara is born

1918—Daughter Eleanor is born

1922—Helps start the Inland Bird-Banding Association

1923—Daughter Janet is born

1924—Margaret and Blaine publish *The Birds of Oklahoma.*

1926—Receives a master's degree in psychology from Clark University for her study of language development

1927—Moves to Columbus, Ohio

1928—Daughter Eleanor dies. Bands first song sparrow, Uno

1933—Publishes *The Theory of Territorialism and Its Development*

1936—Moves to Chicago, Illinois

1937—Publishes *Studies in the Life History of the Song Sparrow*

1937—Becomes the first woman to serve as president of a major American ornithological organization (the Wilson Ornithological Club)

1939—Publishes *The Watcher at the Nest*

1943—Publishes *Studies in the Life History of the Song Sparrow, Volume 2*

1943—Receives the American Ornithologists' Union's Brewster Medal for her song sparrow studies

1962—Publishes the two-volume book *Development of Precocial Behavior in Birds*

1974—Dies on June 26, a few months after Blaine

Margaret receives an honorary doctorate of science degree from Mount Holyoke College, 1955

Glossary

brood: a group of birds hatched together

calls: short notes repeated over and over to send a message

conservationist: a person who protects nature

courtship: the act of trying to attract a mate

endangered: at risk of losing all members of a species forever

naturalist: a person who studies nature

nestling: a young bird that has not yet left the nest

ornithologist: a scientist who studies birds

pesticides: chemicals used to kill "pest" animals such as insects

predators: animals that hunt and eat other animals

range: the area in which an animal is found

song post: a perch from which a bird sings to announce "ownership" of a piece of land

species: a group of plants or animals that are able to breed with one another

territory: an area claimed by a group or individual

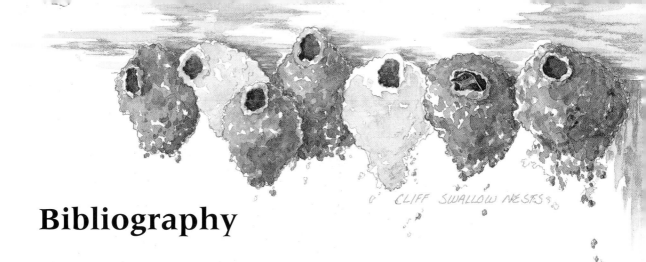

CLIFF SWALLOW NESTS

Bibliography

Bonta, Marcia Myers. "Margaret Morse Nice: Ethologist of the Song Sparrow." *Women in the Field: America's Pioneering Women Naturalists.* College Station, TX: Texas A&M University Press, 1991.

*Dunlap, Julie. *Birds in the Bushes: A Story about Margaret Morse Nice.* Minneapolis: Carolrhoda Books, 1996.

Nice, Margaret Morse. *Development of Behavior in Precocial Birds.* New York: Linnaean Society of New York, 1962.

———. *Research is a Passion with Me.* Toronto: Consolidated Amethyst Communications, 1979.

———. "The Role of Territory in Bird Life." *The American Midland Naturalist* 26 (1941): 441-487.

———. *Studies in the Life History of the Song Sparrow,* vols. 1 and 2, 2nd ed. New York: Dover Publications, 1964.

———. *The Watcher at the Nest.* New York: Macmillan, 1939.

Trautman, Milton. "In Memorium: Margaret Morse Nice." *Auk* 94 (1977): 430-441.

*An asterisk denotes material for younger readers.

Index